Putting a "Lid" on Food-on-the-Stove Fires

**Fire Chief (Ret.) Stan Tarnowski
with
Battalion Chief (Ret.) Robert Avsec**

ISBN: 978-1-365-93734-7

PublishNation LLC
www.publishnation.net

Table of Contents

Foreword

Great Reading!

Fire Chief (Ret.) Stan Tarnowski is a long-time friend and colleague and it gives me great pleasure to provide the foreword to his first eBook, ***Putting a "Lid" on Food-on-the-Stove Fires***. Chief Tarnowski and his editor—another good friend and colleague of mine, Battalion Chief (Ret.) Robert Avsec—have created what is sure to be a "groundbreaking effort" in reducing the number of kitchen fires in the USA.

Putting a "Lid" on Food-on-the-Stove Fires will give any Fire Service leader the information and example necessary to implement their own Fire Prevention Ordinance using High-End Heat-Limiting Technology (HEHLT). This eBook is sure to become a "must read" for all Fire Service leaders looking to reduce the death and destruction of property caused by cooking related fires. (Please keep in mind that cooking fires have been the #1 cause of home fires in the United States for the past 40 years).

Chief Tarnowski's simple, but effective, step-by-step guide is easy to use and implement in your community. The Chief knows what he's talking about because he "walked the walk, and talked the talk" by being a big part of the successful adoption and implementation of a Fire Prevention Ordinance—with HEHLT as its foundation—in Union City, Georgia. I highly recommend ***Putting a "Lid" on Food-on-the-Stove Fires*** for all Fire Officers personal and Departmental libraries!

Fire Chief Dennis Rubin (Ret.)
D.C. Fire Department,
Author – Teacher – Consultant

May 28, 2013

Introduction

My wife—and by proxy me as well—is a huge fan of the crime procedurals that have dominated television in recent years, e.g., NCIS, and CSI (and the NY and Miami spin-offs). A common theme I hear every week is one of the characters telling one of their colleagues (who's usually letting some emotion get in the way of logic), "Follow the evidence."

How well are we in the Fire & EMS business doing at "following the evidence"?

According to a National Fire Protection Association (NFPA) Fact Sheet, U.S. fire departments responded to an estimated average of 371,700 home structure fires per year during 2006-2010. These fires caused an annual average of 2,590 civilian fire deaths, 2,910 civilian fire injuries, and $7.2 billion in direct damage. 92% of all structure fire deaths resulted from home fires. On average, seven people died in U.S. home fires per day during the period.

So What Should We Do?

- 67% of all civilian fire injuries occurred as a result of fires in residential buildings.
- Cooking (30 percent) was the primary cause for residential building fires that resulted in injuries.
- 35% of civilian fire injuries in residential buildings resulted from trying to control a fire followed by attempting to escape (26 percent).
- 79% of injuries resulting from residential building fires involved smoke inhalation and thermal burns.
- The leading human factor contributing to injuries in residential building fires was being asleep—55 percent)
- Bedrooms—35%--were the leading location where civilian injuries occurred in residential building fires.

Civilian Fire Injuries in Residential Buildings (2008-2010)

For starters, we must realize that we cannot eliminate fires, and the resultant deaths and injuries, completely. Not going to happen. At least not until we identify the "stupid" gene in people that leads them to do incredibly dumb things that cause fire. There, I said it. (To quote one of my favorite comics, Ron White, "You can't fix stupid!"

In the 1960's, our society finally had enough of the deaths and destruction from automobile crashes on the highways and by-ways of America. The United States Congress—which used to do its job in things like this!—enacted the National Traffic and Motor Vehicle Safety Act in 1966:

The National Traffic and Motor Vehicle Safety Act empowered the federal government to set and administer new safety standards for motor vehicles and road traffic safety. The Act created the National Highway Safety Bureau (now National Highway Traffic Safety Administration). The Act was the government's response to increasing number of cars and associated fatalities and injuries on the road following a period when the number of people killed on the road had increased 6-fold and the number of vehicles was up 11-fold since 1925.

The reduction of the rate of death attributable to motor-vehicle crashes in the United States represents the successful public health response to a great technologic advance of the 20th century—the motorization of America.

How did it happen? We as a society took a systematic approach to solving the problem that resulted in changes such as:

1. Birth of the modern trauma care and Emergency Medical Services in the United States.

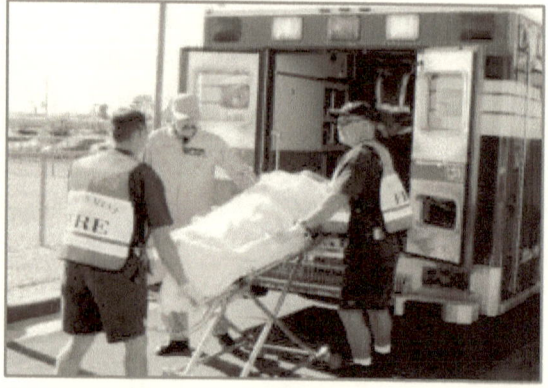

2

2. Engineering changes to automobiles to protect occupants: lap/shoulder belt restraint systems; air bag restraint systems; energy-absorbing steering columns; vehicle chassis construction that dissipates crash energy to protect vehicle occupants.

3. Improved road construction design included: guard rails to prevent vehicles from striking stationary objects, e.g., bridge abutments, and vehicles from leaving the road, e.g., tight curves, and crossing into on-coming traffic.

So Why Aren't We Taking the Same Approach to Preventable Fires?

The United States has known it's had a fire problem since at least 1948, when President Harry S. Truman received the Report of the Continuing Committee of the President's Conference on Fire Prevention and Education. Our 33rd president responded to the report by stating:

The serious losses in life and property resulting annually from fires cause me deep concern. I am sure that such unnecessary waste can be reduced. The substantial progress made in the science of fire prevention and fire protection in this country during the past forty years convinces me that the means are available for limiting this unnecessary destruction.

The authors of that report, along with the participants at the five Wingspread symposiums since — ***Wingspread Conference on Fire Service Administration, Education and Research*** (1966), Wingspread II (1976), III (1986), IV (1996), and V (2003) — have all said the same thing when it comes to addressing the fire problem in America:

Fire prevention and accident prevention employ same technique. –
Over the years, the approaches to the accident problem have been
popularly designated as the Three E's of Safety – Engineering,
Enforcement, and Education. These 'Three E's' are equally applicable
to fire prevention and protection.

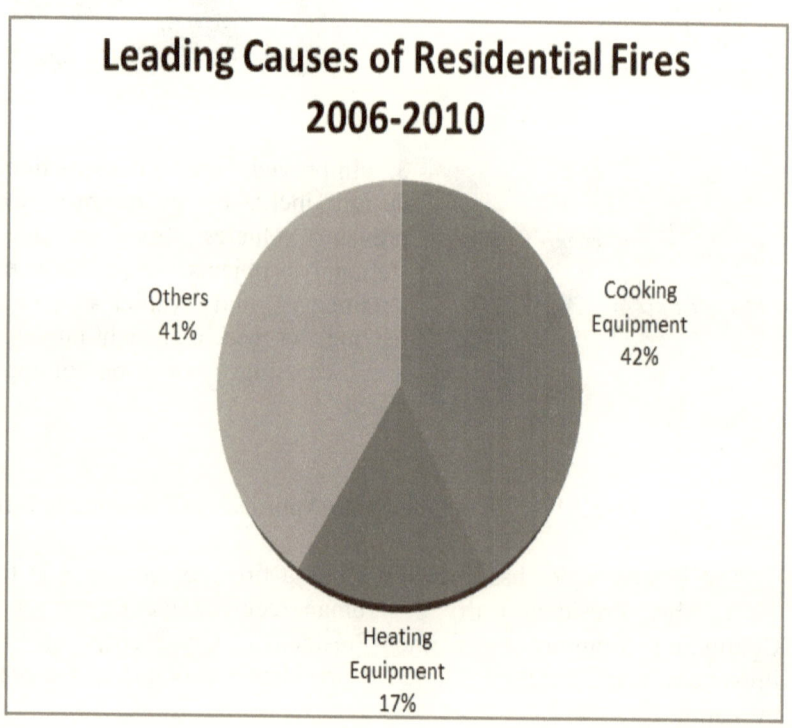

Homes include one- or two-family homes, manufactured homes, as
well as apartments or other multi-family housing. In general, any fire
that occurs in a structure is considered a structure fire, even if the fire
was limited to contents and the building itself was not damaged. The
predominant causes of residential fires in the United States for the
period are Cooking Equipment and Heating Equipment. Other fires
include: Intentional (8%); Electrical Distribution and Lighting (6%);
Smoking (5%); Clothes washers and dryers (4%); Exposures (3%);
Candles (3%); and Playing with fire (2%).

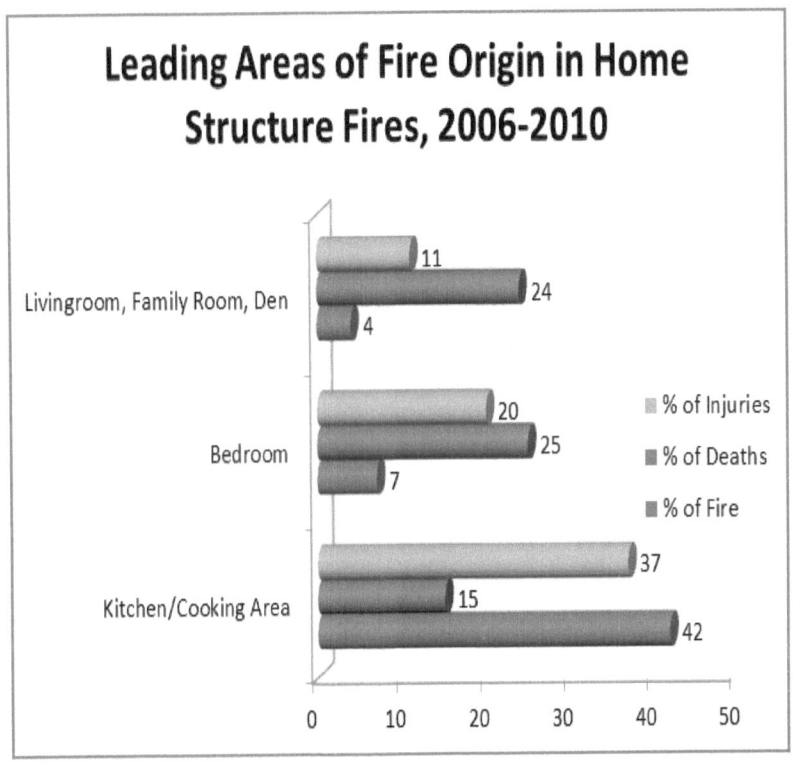

Leading Areas of Fire Origin in Home Structure Fires, 2006-2010

Livingroom, Family Room, Den
- 11
- 24
- 4

Bedroom
- 20
- 25
- 7

Kitchen/Cooking Area
- 37
- 15
- 42

- ▪ % of Injuries
- ▪ % of Deaths
- ▪ % of Fire

The Kitchen/Cooking Area accounts for the highest percentage of both fires and fire injuries. Though they only account for a combined 11% of all fires, the Bedroom and Living Areas (Living room, Family Room, or Den) are where 49% of fire deaths occur.

If we took the same approach to reducing the number of fires and their impact on our society we'd push for changes like these:

Action Item: All residential cooking equipment manufactured and installed in homes would come equipped with a fire suppression system installed, e.g., a hood suppression system. That system would also shut down the fuel supply to the equipment upon activation of the system.

Impact: The greatest source of fires, in the most frequent location of origin (42%), would be "stopped in its tracks": (1) in its incipient stage before it could spread; and (2) occupant's would not be injured (37% of fire injuries) attempting to extinguish the fire or attempting to remove a burning pot from the stove.

Action Item: Require the installation of partial residential sprinkler coverage in all living areas (living room, family room, and den) and in all bedrooms.

Impact: Fires would be controlled in their incipient stage in the residential areas that account for the largest percentage of civilian fire deaths (combined 49%) and second leading area for civilian fire injuries (combined 33%).

These are just two that immediately come to mind when looking at the stats in Figures 1 and 2 above. But if we could be successful in doing this, in a generation or two we could have a substantial positive impact on:

- The Number of Fires (53% that occur in kitchen/cooking areas and living areas);
- The Number of Civilian Fire Deaths (64% that occur in kitchen/cooking areas and living areas); and
- The Number of Civilian Fire Injuries (68% that occur in kitchen/cooking areas and living areas.

Sound rather harsh? Sound unrealistic? Consider for a moment what has happened since 9/11 to fight the "war on terror" – creation of DHS and TSA, hundreds of billions of dollars spent, laws adopted and changed, new training, new equipment, and new ways to do our jobs. With all that and more, we've not suffered a single terrorist-related death or injury on United States soil since that day. We have, however, lost a "city" of 30,966 people (total U.S. fire deaths for 2002-2011) in that same period.

Consequences of not extinguishing a kitchen fire during the fire's incipient (formative) stage. Kitchen fires can rapidly grow and extend beyond the kitchen because of the large amount of combustible materials that are typically in close proximity to the stove top.

But what if we could do even better than what I've proposed? What if we could:

- Stop the stove top fire from ever starting?
- Install after-market technology on electric stoves to prevent stove top fires for less than $400 per stove?
- Install that after-market technology in less than 30 minutes?

It's no longer a case of "what if?" In this eBook, Chief Stan Tarnowski is going to show you how High-End, Heat-Limiting (HEHLT) can be the "silver bullet" in your quest to eliminate residential fires that originate on the stove top of an electric range in your community. Chief Tarnowski and I know that you can do it because he was part of the successful effort to incorporate HEHLT into a Fire Prevention Ordinance that was adopted and implemented by Union City, Georgia and its fire department in September 2012.

Robert Avsec
Battalion Chief (Ret.)
Chesterfield County (VA) Fire & EMS Department

Chapter I

The Food-on-the-Stove Fire

Do any these terms sound familiar to you and the people in your department?

I know they sound familiar to me and probably most fire department personnel across our nation and beyond. The unfortunate fact of life is that where there is cooking going on, there is potential for a "stove top fire".

The National Fire Protection Association, the Federal Emergency Management Agency and many other statistical gathering organizations continue to report that cooking fires are the #1 cause of fire in the United States. This is not new "news": It has been pretty much a steadfast trend over the past 20-plus years. As our country continues to "find its way" to a 21st-century economy, we might well expect this trend to continue.

Many communities continue to see increased development of multi-family dwellings (MFD), a greater percentage of single-family dwellings (SFD) used as rental properties, and a rapid increase in senior citizen population living in both SFD and MFD occupancies. Statistically all of these occupancies and populations have been shown to be at a higher risk for the occurrence of cooking fires.

> **Fact**
>
> From 2008 to 2010, an estimated average of 164,500 cooking fires in residential buildings occurred in the United States each year and resulted in an estimated annual average of 110 deaths, 3,525 injuries, and $309 million in property loss.
>
> The term cooking fires includes those fires that were caused by stoves, ovens, fixed and portable warming units, deep fat fryers, and open grills, as well as those fires that are confined to the cooking vessel.

In today's fiscal climate, every fire department's budget has been trimmed and trimmed to a point that there definitely is no more "fat". Even in the "best of times" (fiscally speaking), a fire department that dedicated even 10 percent of its total budget toward fire prevention and education would have been a "statistical outlier."

When the typical fire department's budget gets cut, fire prevention and public education programs are typically among the first to have their resources slashed or the program is eliminated altogether.

> *One definition of insanity? Repeatedly doing something that has an undesirable outcome the same way, while expecting a different outcome.*

How many times every week do your firefighters respond to the following scenario?

Act 1: Occupant decides to deep fry--using oil or grease--some chicken, fish, or french fries for dinner;

Act 2: While involved in this culinary task, the "cook" gets a phone call or text message, begins a conversation, and wanders away from the kitchen;

Act 3: The next thing they know, they smell smoke—or better yet, hear a smoke detector sounding its alert---and rush to the kitchen only to see a flaming pot on the stove top;

Act 4: The occupant attempts to extinguish the fire by directing water at the fire which in turn splatters the burning liquid and rapidly spreads the fire;

Act 4 (Alternate Action): The occupant grabs the pot from the stove to remove it from the house only to be burned by the flames which causes them to drop the pot which spreads flaming liquid across the kitchen floor;

Act 5 (The Finale): Flames in the kitchen continue to spread, crawling over the ceiling to the adjacent rooms, while everyone hopefully gets out and is calling 911 to get the FD to respond to their "house on fire".

National Estimates of Residential Building Cooking Fires and Losses by Year

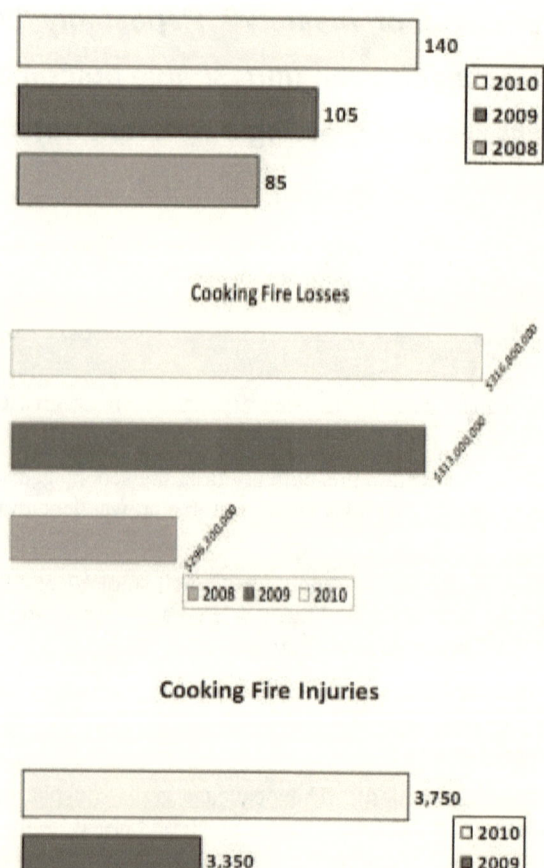

Cooking Fire Deaths

- 140
- 105
- 85

Legend: □ 2010, ■ 2009, ▣ 2008

Cooking Fire Losses

- $314,000,000
- $313,000,000
- $296,100,000

Legend: ▣ 2008, ■ 2009, □ 2010

Cooking Fire Injuries

- 3,750
- 3,350
- 3,475

Legend: □ 2010, ■ 2009, ▣ 2008

Source: National Fire Incident Reporting System (NFRIS)

10

The National Fire Incident Reporting System (NFIRS) was launched by the National Fire Data Center of the United States Fire Administration (USFA), a division of the Federal Emergency Management Agency. The System was established following the Federal Fire Prevention and Control Act of 1974 (P.L. 93-498), which authorizes the USFA to gather and analyze information on the magnitude of the Nation's fire problem, as well as its detailed characteristics and trends. The Act further authorizes the USFA to develop uniform data reporting methods, and to encourage and assist state agencies in developing and reporting data.

The trend is not a good one based on the information and statistics gathered from NFIRS year after year. In my 30 years being in the fire service business, I continue to hear:

- "Well there is nothing we can do about that."
- "What can be done about people carelessly cooking?"
- "We can't force people to pay attention while they are cooking."
- "How can we stop the stove top cooking fire if we are not there?"

All wonderful rationalizations for us to not "think outside the box", right? Well, I will share some information with you in the coming chapters that I hope will convince you that there is *something that you and every department in every community can do!*

Technology is a wonderful thing! We think of technology as our laptop, desk top, iPad, iPhone, e-reader, and all other modes of info gathering and sharing resources in our daily lives. But technology that helps us do our job needn't stop there. Thanks to some leading edge design technicians in the private sector, we now have cooking appliance technology that can help us to effectively make cooking fires—particularly those that result from deep frying—a thing of the past. Seriously.

I'm going to share technology with you that has been designed, manufactured, rigorously tested by the appropriate testing agencies, approved and put in the field to make elimination of stove top cooking fires a reality in our lifetime. (The Mayor and City Council of Union City, Georgia, for one, enacted a city-wide ordinance in September 2012 that mandates the use of this technology).

Before we get to the tool, let's take a minute to examine the "chain of events" that results in a stove top cooking fire. Take a look at the following picture:

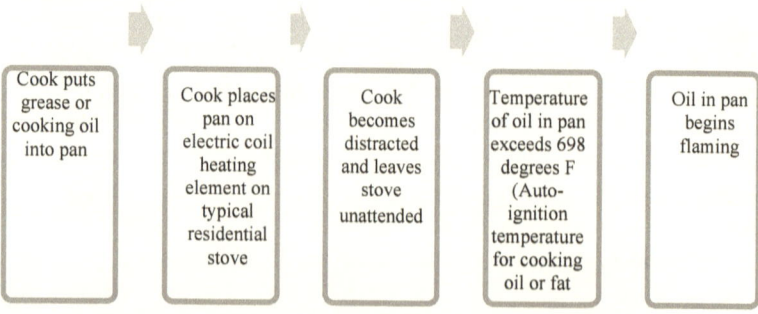

The Progression of a Typical Cooking Fire Resulting from Deep Frying Cooking.

Residential electric stove elements deliver more than 698 degrees F of heat to the burners; some are capable of 1,300 to 1,600 degrees F. (well above the 698 Degree F needed to ignite other ordinary class A combustibles).

Now, let's say that we could provide a simple, yet effective, mechanism to control/limit the highest heat to any of the four heating elements on the stove top so that their temperature would never, ever exceed 668 degrees F. This temperature is sufficient enough to heat oil or grease to a proper temperature for frying, but never enough to reach the 698 degrees F required for auto-ignition of the cooking oil or grease. That's exactly what High-End, Heat-Limiting Technology (HEHLT) does when properly installed.

What is HEHLT? Read on, because it's coming at you in Chapter II!

Chapter II

High-End, Heat-Limiting Technology (HEHLT)

The Safe-T-Element® is a HEHLT device that replaces the existing heating coils of the range and adds a thermocouple control circuit for each burner. These thermocouple circuits prevent the coils from reaching the auto-ignition temperatures of cooking oils (370°C/698°F) or common household cellulose materials (400°C/752°F). There is still plenty of heat available to cook the food (and even blacken it), but unattended cooking can no longer start a kitchen fire.

How about that? No fire to start, regardless of how long the person is away from the stove top or how long the oil has been heating up. HEHLT is a reality and available to everyone who has an electric coil stove top and it's affordable at less than $300 per stove top (four elements). The technology meets National Electrical Code requirements, is installed in over 85,000 homes in the United States today, and is recognized by, among others, the International Association of Fire Chiefs (IAFC) and the Department of Defense (DoD). (DoD has mandated the installation of HEHLT in all military residential housing on DoD facilities world-wide).

As you continue reading, you will learn more about the technology and how your department can become "fully involved" as fire prevention and fire safety activists, without spending large sums of money. By the time we get done, you will have the information and knowledge that you need to start the journey towards the eradication of cooking fires in your community.

When it comes to reducing any fire incident, not just food on the stove (FOS) fires, we have five accepted strategies at our disposal:

Education: Teaching the public and responders what risks threaten their community and what they can do to help prevent and/or mitigate the impact;

Engineering: Suggesting the use of technology, such as smoke alarms and residential sprinklers, to help prevent and/or mitigate target risks;

Enforcement: Passing, strengthening and enforcing codes, laws and ordinances;

Economic incentive: Working to incorporate incentives that support risk reduction such as tax incentives for installation of residential sprinklers or free smoke alarms; and

Emergency response: Support the existence of an adequately staffed, equipped and trained group of emergency responders.

Source: National Fire Academy. Coffee Break Training—Fire Prevention and Public Education. *Leading a Fire Prevention/Risk-Reduction Bureau*. No. FM-2013-2, April 4, 2013.

HEHLT is a great example of how we can provide an "engineering" solution to FOS fires. By having the equipment installed directly on the stove's electric coils, the technology is "on the job" whenever the element is energized. Thus, the system controls the excessive heat for the occupant, even if they are not giving their full attention to their assignment, cooking!

Take a look at the components below and also view a video of how the Safe-T-Element™ prevents these fires.

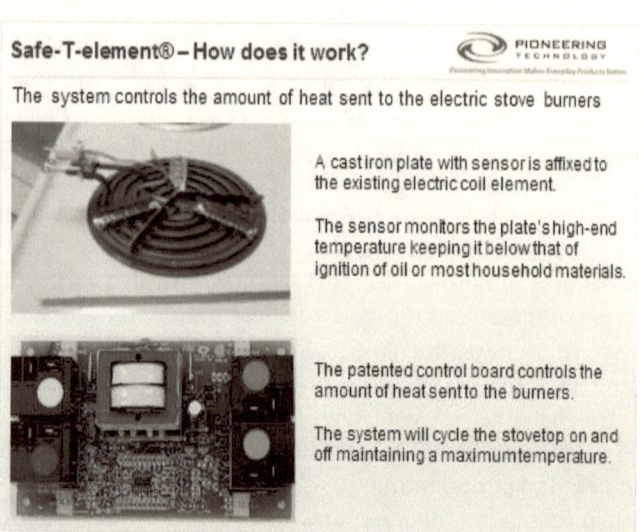

The Safe-T-Element™ is now available on new stoves and can be retrofitted on existing electric stove heating elements.

Now, more than ever, we as fire service professionals must take advantage of this new engineered solution for FOS fires. We can have a positive influence on the reduction of FOS fires by aggressively marketing this solution to our local government officials and the general public, more so than we're currently having with trying to create a more informed and educated public.

Using our limited resources, we must promote the use of this technology that doesn't just extinguish a fire after it starts, like a hood system or sprinkler system, but actually prevents the fire from starting at all! The message is simple:

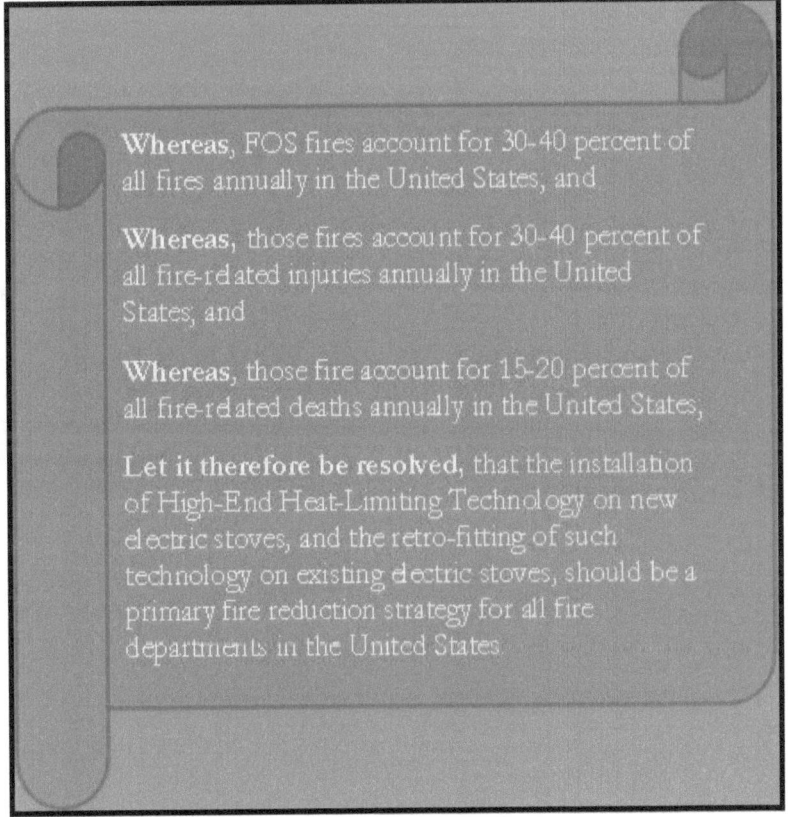

Whereas, FOS fires account for 30-40 percent of all fires annually in the United States, and

Whereas, those fires account for 30-40 percent of all fire-related injuries annually in the United States; and

Whereas, those fire account for 15-20 percent of all fire-related deaths annually in the United States;

Let it therefore be resolved, that the installation of High-End Heat-Limiting Technology on new electric stoves, and the retro-fitting of such technology on existing electric stoves, should be a primary fire reduction strategy for all fire departments in the United States

What impact would we have on FOS if every community in the USA adopted this resolution?

We must start by educating "our own", e.g., the members of our individual Fire & EMS departments, so they truly understand the *Why, What, and How* behind this engineered solution for FOS fires. Next, we need to develop a program to inform and educate our local government officials, e.g., city managers, county managers, city council members, county commissioners, etc., using the same message to obtain their support to enact appropriate legislation, ordinances, codes, etc.

Finally, we must develop strategies to inform and educate those who are responsible for the operation and management of multi-family affordable housing complexes, multi-residential senior's facilities, housing authorities, military housing, university/college housing, extended stay hotels, and facilities that house those who are mentally or physically challenged, to name a few. We know that, statistically, the populations that are most at risk for having a FOS fire live in these occupancies.

FOS fires are serious business for a community fire department to manage. It takes a lot of resources to effectively extinguish a stove top kitchen fire after the fact. We could better dedicate our precious resources toward efforts to prevent non-FOS fires, aka, the "other" 60-70 percent of fires in our communities if we make high-end heat-limiting technology the new standard for electric stoves.

What do you think? Are you ready to learn how to take this technology and message and start putting a "lid" on food-on-the-stove fires in your community?

Then let's get started!

Chapter III

Developing a Strategy for Reducing FOS Fires using HEHLT

Let's talk about a "game plan" that you can use to begin your internal and external marketing efforts to win support for this amazing technology. When I served as the Fire Chief in Union City, Georgia, we had a placard on the side of our 100-foot E-One Tower that displayed our department: *Dedicated to Excellence & Determined to Make a Difference"!* You have to live it, to make a difference, everyday!

In the previous chapter we discussed the five accepted strategies that have to be addressed if we want to have a positive impact on reducing the frequency and severity of fires in the USA. Our discussion is now going to move on to how you can create an effective strategy for reducing the number of FOS fires in your community. By doing so, you and your department can make a significant difference in how the general public will be able to prevent FOS fires, fires that cause such destruction in the lives of millions every year.

Since not everyone thinks like a firefighter, it is incumbent upon us, those who are firefighters, to continue on our mission to enhance our fire safety and fire prevention initiatives within our organizational structure and in our communities!

In the 21st century fire service, we are expected to be a service that is ready to handle "any and all hazards" responses. Most people are confident that when they dial 911, what will arrive are firefighters totally equipped to handle and mitigate their emergency. However, in the current environment where budgets and staffing for our services are continually being reduced we must aggressively move forward at finding ways to work smarter, not harder. HEHLT is a proven technology that can help us do just that because it gives us a tool that:

- Effectively prevents a FOS fire from happening on an electric stove where it is installed;
- The cost of the technological solution to FOS fires is borne by the owner of the dwelling where the stove is located; and

- Effectively reduces the frequency of the most common cause of residential fires in the USA (unattended cooking) thus reducing the number of such fires that require a fire department response.

If we are successful in such an endeavor, we will develop an equally confident attitude on their part that we are doing everything in our power to prevent fires from ever happening.

I've introduced a new technology that can have a dramatic impact on the number of fires that result from unattended cooking on an electric range stovetop, HEHLT. The next chapter will provide an actual case study of how HEHLT was incorporated into the fire reductions strategies for a local government and its fire department.

Chapter IV

Union City, Georgia Adopts HEHLT Ordinance (Case Study)

The following is a case study that looks at how the Union City (GA) Fire Department (located 20 minutes south of downtown Atlanta) successfully introduced this new technology into their community in September 2012.

Union City Fire Department staffs three stations with full-time career firefighters and provides fire suppression, EMS (BLS and ALS levels of service), and rescue services. The Fire Prevention Bureau is led by a Fire Marshal (Battalion Chief rank) who is a direct report to the Fire Chief. (Our discussions here, i.e., the sequence of events and timelines, will of course include a larger audience for larger organizations, larger communities, and more diverse communities, but the concepts and procedures should remain the same).

In every successful company or organization, we know that it takes the entire TEAM effort to bring any new program or initiative to fruition. Below are the initial steps we took in Union City:

Step 1: Problem Identification

Any new idea, product, tool, process, system, service, etc., that we in the fire service come up with, will never come to fruition unless we put it into a recommended evaluation process or cycle. In this case, the Fire Chief, Deputy Chief, Fire Marshall, all Operations Commanders, Captains, Lieutenants, and firefighters of all tenured levels understood that over 95 percent of their residential structure fires had originated from "unattended cooking on the stove" over the last four decades.

Step 2: Identify Potential Solution to the Problem

Department personnel, including the Fire Chief, became aware of "HEHLT" (High-End Heat-Limiting Technology) that was designed to prevent an unattended "stove top pan fire" from occurring. When properly installed as a replacement for the standard electric stovetop heating element, HEHLT prevents the element temperature from reaching the 698 degrees F, the auto-ignition temperature of common cooking oils. This was an ideal situation and it underscores the necessity of having "buy-in" from throughout the organization.

Step 3: Getting Local Government "on board"

We conducted briefing sessions with the Mayor and City Council members of Union City to inform and educate them about HEHLT and its potential to have a positive impact on the leading cause of fires in Union City. We showed them the technology and its supporting documentation.

We also gave them concrete examples of how other Authorities Having Jurisdiction (AHJ) had successfully "bundled" three of the "5-E's"—Engineering, Enforcement, and Economic Incentives—into ordinance changes.

Step 4: Getting Customer "buy-in"

The Union City Fire Marshal then met with all community residential managers that would fall under the new ordinance mandate. Together company representatives for the HEHLT, the Fire Marshal delivered presentations—that included a "table top" demonstration showing how the HEHLT prevented a stove top fire, alongside a fire occurring on a stove element without HEHLT installed—to community stakeholder groups. (A real "WOW" moment!).

At the conclusion of the demonstration, we handed out a questionnaire to the residential managers present to determine how likely they believed that HEHLT was a tool that would prevent fire and property damage and make their residents feel safer. The residential managers in Union City had a lot of experience in dealing with property loss from stove top fires and their questionnaire responses strongly supported the enactment of a city-wide ordinance to embrace the use of HEHLT.

Step 5: Write, Approve, and Enact the Ordinance

In the Union City case, it took approximately 60 days to get from the first meeting—involving the Fire Department leadership, the Mayor, and City Council—to the adoption of the city-wide ordinance requiring the installation of HEHLT on all electric-coil cooking devices located in all tax-supported housing, apartments, triplexes, residential board and care occupancies, small nursing homes, convalescent homes, assisted-living occupancies within the Union City. (The entire ordinance follows beginning on the next full page).

BE IT ORDAINED BY THE CITY COUNCIL OF UNION CITY:

SECTION 1. That in Chapter (6) of the City Code, entitled "Fire Prevention and Protection", Article II, entitled "Fire Prevention Code" that a new subsection 6-23, entitled "Electric Cooking Devices in Tax-Supported Housing, Apartments, Tri-Plex, Residual Board and Care Occupancies, ,Small Nursing Homes, Convalescent Homes, Assistant Living Occupancies " be incorporated as follows:

All electric coil cooking devices in said housing shall be equipped with listed and approved high end heat limiting technology as recommended by the Fire Marshal, or Authority Having Jurisdiction. Initial requirement will be for this technology on all new coil type electric ranges purchased for the purpose of replacement in existing housing, or as standard equipment for all new tax supported housing Apartments, Tri-Plex, Residual Board and Care Occupancies, Small Nursing Homes, Convalescent Homes, Assistant Living Occupancies, being built. All electric coil type ranges in all existing tax supported housing, Apartments, Tri-Plex, Residual Board and Care Occupancies, Small Nursing Homes, Convalescent Homes, Assistant Living Occupancies must comply with this requirement by the end of 2016.

Definitions:

1. Electric Coil Cooking Devices: All cooking devices that utilize a coil for the cooking heat source. This includes free standing and built in electric ranges, "drop in" type counter-top cook tops and hot plates.
2. High End Heat Limiting Technology: A device that is hard wired into the electric coil range (tamper proof) that limits the high end cooking temperature to a safe level that prevents auto-ignition of common cooking and household materials.
3. Tax Supported Housing: Any housing that is initially constructed by, and/or rent subsidized by the taxpayers for the purpose of providing affordable housing for the at-need citizens within the Union City jurisdiction. Also included are privately owned properties for the purpose of rental, in which the rent is subsidized by the taxpayers.

4. Apartments Building: A building or portion thereof containing three or more dwelling units with independent cooking and bathroom facilities.
5. Residential Board and Care Occupancy: A building or portion thereof that is used for lodging and boarding of four or more residents, not related by blood or marriage to the owners or operators, for the purpose of providing personal care services.

Residential Board and Care Occupancy. The following are examples of facilities that are classified as residential board and care occupancies:

1. Group housing arrangement for physically or mentally handicapped persons who normally attend school in the community, attend worship in the community, or otherwise use community facilities
2. Group housing arrangement for physically or mentally handicapped persons who are undergoing training in preparation for independent living, for paid employment, or for other normal community activities
3. Group housing arrangement for the elderly that provides personal care services but that does not provide nursing care
4. Facilities for social rehabilitation, alcoholism, drug abuse, or mental health problems that contain a group housing arrangement and that provide personal care services but do not provide acute care
5. Assisted living facilities
6. Nursing Home. A building or portion of a building used on a 24-hour basis for the housing and nursing care of four or more persons who, because of mental or physical incapacity, might be unable to provide for their own needs and safety without the assistance of another person.

SECTION 2. That this ordinance may be enforced by any one, all, or a combination of the remedies authorized

SECTION 3. That all ordinances or parts of ordinances, in conflict with this ordinance are hereby repealed to the extent of such conflict.

SECTION 4. That if any section, subsection, paragraph, sentence, clause, phrase, or portion of this ordinance is for any reason held invalid or unconstitutional by a court of competent jurisdiction, such portion shall be deemed severable and such holding shall not affect the validity of the remaining portions hereof.

SECTION 5. That this ordinance shall become effective immediately upon its adoption.

DULY ADOPTED this _____ day of _____, 2012.

Chapter V

Creating a FOS Fire Reduction Strategy
for Your Community

Forty years ago, on May 4, 1973, the National Commission on Fire Prevention and Control delivered the seminal fire service report, America Burning, to President Richard M. Nixon. After two years of exhaustive work the commission members produced a report that provided an unvarnished evaluation of the fire problem in the USA, along with a comprehensive set of recommendations for reducing the loss of human life and property from hostile fire.

The USFA [United States Fire Administration] has recently adopted a new rallying cry of "fire is everyone's fight," a slogan that underscores the opening line of America Burning: "The striking aspect of the Nation's fire problem is the indifference with which Americans confront the subject." As the USFA says, we rely on the fire service to fight fires once they occur, but the prevention of fires is up to all of us. Marty Ahrens, Senior Manager in Fire Analysis & Research Division at NFPA, *America Burning 1973-2013: A Work in Progress*, NFPA Journal May/June 2013.

While America Burning changed our perceptions—those of the fire service for sure, the general public not so much—about the many aspects of fire in this country, we still have much work to do 40 years later.

It has been my objective in developing this eBook to provide every reader, with a step-by-step guide, and the valuable tools to reduce the frequency and severity of FOS fires. Let's take a look below at the most current NFPA News Release, which details the fire statistics and data relative to home structure fires in the years 2007-2011, which show that these fires are still "leading the pack."

NFPA Press Release (April 23, 2013) states that: (*Lorraine Carli-Public Affairs Office*)

Causes and Circumstances of Home Fires

Cooking equipment was the leading cause of home structure fires and home fire injuries (And has been for the past 20+ years).

63% of the range or stove top fires beginning with food, occurred when someone was frying (Source: U.S. Consumer Product Safety Commission)

A study published by the U.S. Consumer Product Safety Commission found that:

- 75% of range or stove fires started with food ignitions.
- 43% began with cooking oil,
- 33% started with fish or meat.

I have always struggled to understand why these statistics for some

reason haven't changed much over the past 20+ years. Why do we continue to see an overall rise in kitchen/cooking fires? My unofficial polling of many department chiefs from across the country leads me to believe that many of us have become "conditioned" into thinking that our community will always suffer these types of fires due to carelessness of the home cooks (You can't fix stupid!).

So we continue to try our best—with the limited resources available—to provide our "standardized" educational programs through a variety of mediums:

- Informational pamphlets and handouts;
- School fire prevention programs for the children to bring back word to the parents;
- Public service announcements on the local cable TV channel;
- Fire department banners and placards; and
- Social media outreach via Twitter, Facebook, Pintrest, etc.

This has been our mode of operation for as long as I have been connected to the fire service, some 30 years. Not to say that it is bad, because when you work to inform and educate the citizen base that is one of the "5-E's" that we should be doing. But what about the other four E's?

HEHLT (High End Heat Limiting Technology)

With HEHLT installed on the stove top, the owner or occupant has significantly reduced the potential for a fire to start in the kitchen where: Two of every five (42%) reported home structure fires started. These fires caused more than one-third (38%) of civilian home fire injuries. And, 16% of home fire deaths also resulted from kitchen fires.

Example of a HEHLT replacement element

Enter HEHLT, affordable technology that easily replaces existing electric coil stove top elements, the stove type used by a majority of the general population. With this single piece of technology we now have a tool to address the remaining four of the "5-E's".

We now have a tool that has the potential to "slay the dragon" (provide a meaningful reduction in the frequency and severity of fire) that can—dare I say it?—be better than residential fire sprinklers.

Heresy, you say? Consider this: when a fire sprinkler is "called upon" to do its job it means a fire has started. After the sprinkler does its job the owner or occupant still has a clean-up and restoration problem, albeit MUCH smaller than if the sprinkler had not been present. With HEHLT installed on the stove top, the owner or occupant has significantly reduced the potential for a fire to start in the kitchen.

If we in the leadership of Fire & EMS organizations embrace this new technology—which has already been done successfully at the local, state, and federal levels in various locations across the USA—we can "bring life" to all five of the "5-E's". Take a look at the chart on the next page to see how it all "matches up".

The Five "E's" of Fire Prevention & Reduction	What HEHLT Adds
Education: Teaching the public and responders what risks threaten their community and what they can do to help prevent and/or mitigate the impact.	With the use of the HEHLT on electric coil burners, cooking oils and food cannot reach the auto-ignition temperatures needed for flame production, therefore no flame spread, (no fire).
Engineering: Suggesting the use of technology, such as smoke alarms and residential sprinklers, to help prevent and/or mitigate target risks.	The HEHLT technology is engineered to be easily and safely installed without great expense and prevents the fire from occurring.
Enforcement: Passing, strengthening and enforcing codes, laws and ordinances.	The adoption of a new or amended Fire Safety/Prevention Code in your government jurisdiction (like Union City, Georgia did) will drive this initiative.
Economic incentive: Working to incorporate incentives that support risk reduction such as tax incentives for installation of residential sprinklers or free smoke alarms.	The HEHLT is approved for developers/builders to use where they can receive points up to 4 when they are applying for Tax Credit funding (QAP) at the state & local level when building residential buildings that are partially government funded such as: low income housing; Section 8 housing; assisted living facilities; and retirement communities. (These are also the high risk occupancy types and populations—for most communities—that are most adversely affected by stove top fires in the kitchen).
Emergency response: Support the existence of an adequately staffed, equipped and trained group of emergency responders.	Many of our Departments have experienced serious budget cuts, which leads to not filling vacant positions or even having to furlough folks, which puts us in compromising situations. By having fewer kitchen/food on the stove fires that can quickly escalate into more serious fires, our personnel are less at risk and ready for other type fires and calls.

Conclusion

When I first learned of HEHLT, my first thought was: I have to present this technology to the Union City Fire Department. I had been the Fire Chief in Union City and felt strongly that the current leadership would be very excited to see how they could adopt it in Union City to reduce fires and subsequent injuries and fatalities from these types of fires which they were very familiar with over the years.

The Union City Fire Department under the Direction of Chief Donald Leasher, and their Fire Marshal, Battalion Chief Larry Knowles, successfully used the five-step process that I've presented in this four-part blog series to pass a City Ordinance which mandates the use of the HEHLT.

I know that the personnel at the Union City Fire Department are very proud that they have been able to think and reach "outside the box" to implement a system that will reduce stove top fires in the kitchens of Union City. I hope that with this blog series I've been able to give you and your organization the "tools" to make it happen in your community.

Until next time, be safe!
Chief T

About the Authors

Fire Chief (Ret.) Stan Tarnowski began his career in 1975 with the Boston (MA) Logan International Airport Fire Department serving in multiple operational and administrative positions. In Metro Atlanta, Georgia, he served as fire chief, 911 and EMA director in Union City, deputy and suppression chief at the Georgia State Academy and chief of training at the Henry County Fire Department. Tarnowski received his associate's degree in fire science in 1976 from Bunker Hill Community College, holds several public safety certifications, and is an NPQ Board Certified Level 4 fire instructor. He is currently the president of Firesafe Consulting Group.

Battalion Chief Robert Avsec (Ret.) served with the Chesterfield (Va.) Fire & EMS Department for 26 years. He was an active instructor for fire, EMS, and hazardous materials courses at the local, state, and federal levels, which included more than 10 years with the National Fire Academy. Chief Avsec earned his undergraduate degree from the University of Cincinnati and his Master of Science degree in Executive Fire Service Leadership from Grand Canyon University. He is a 2001 graduate of the National Fire Academy's Executive Fire Officer Program.

Appendices

(Hint? Make sure you get to Appendix I for an extra special treat!)

Appendix A: Toronto (Canada) Community Housing Case Study

 **safeТelement®**
helps prevent cooking fires before they start   **Case Study – Public Housing**

"Stove-top Cooking Fires Eliminated at Toronto Community Housing"

Toronto
Community
Housing

Toronto Community Housing (TCH) is the largest social housing provider in Canada and the second largest in North America. TCH is home to about 164,000 low and moderate-income tenants in 58,500 households (seniors, families, singles, refugees, recent immigrants to Canada and people with special needs) – 6% of the city's population.

The mandate of Toronto Community Housing is to provide quality housing for low and moderate income households and to create community conditions that minimize risk and promote resiliency.

The Problem

Stove top cooking is the "Number One cause of household fire" in North America. Cooking left unattended is the number one reason for these fires.

According to the Canadian Fire Safety Association cooking equipment was identified as the leading ignition source attributed to preventable home fires in Ontario, averaging 1,494 fires annually or 24% of all preventable home fires.

But some of the most shocking statistics reveal that 43.4% of all stovetop fires occur in multi-unit residences and that 63.2% of stovetop fires are in subsidized units (The Office of the Ontario Fire Marshal).

The cause of these fires is typically related to unattended cooking, that is the cook turns on the stove and leaves the room or the housing unit while cooking.

Oil left unattended can quickly ignite and result in a grease fire. These grease fires tend to accelerate quickly spreading beyond the vicinity of the stove (cabinets, curtains, floors etc.).

Toronto Community Housing Cooking Fires 2005-10		
Year	# of cooking fires	$ Cost
2010 (as of July/10)	19	$ 312,000
2009	28	$ 574,000
2008	23	$ 489,000
2007	17	$ 233,000
2006	24	$ 489,000
2005	20	$ 117,000
Total	131 (as of Jul/10)	$ 2,214,000

- Unattended cooking is the primary cause of TCH fires.
- Cooking fires primarily occur when pots of cooking oil are left on stovetops in unattended kitchens.
- Approx. 9% of TCH tenants suffer from mental illness
- *"In the 131 Cooking fires at TCH I do not recall an instance where a tenant was in the kitchen cooking when the fire began"* – Brian Laur (Risk Management)
- TCH experienced one death & several injuries.

 PIONEERING
TECHNOLOGY

Appendix B: U.S. Universities that have installed HEHLT

Appendix C: U.S. Housing Authorities Using Safe-T-element® Technology

 PIONEERING TECHNOLOGY

U.S. Housing Authorities with the Safe-T-element® Technology

1. Atlantic American Partners, LLC — RI
2. Avalon Housing, Inc. — MI
3. Bay County — MI
4. Bloomington Housing Authority — IL
5. Boulder Housing Authority — CO
6. Boyd Management — SC
7. Brevard County Housing Authority — FL
8. Buffalo Housing Authority — NY
9. Floyd County Housing Authority — KY
10. Grand Junction Housing Authority — CO
11. Green Bay Housing Authority — WI
12. Housing Authority of Clallam County — WA
13. Housing Authority of the City of Winston-Salem — NC
14. Housing Authority of Union — SC
15. Kankakee Housing Authority — IL
16. King County Housing Authority — WA
17. Lakeland Housing Authority — FL
18. Logan County Housing Authority — IL
19. Macoupin County Housing Authority — IL
20. New Albany Housing Authority — IN
21. Newport News Housing Authority — VA
22. Norfolk Redevelopment & Housing Authority — VA
23. North Charleston Housing Authority — SC
24. Peoria Housing Authority — IL
25. Pittsfield Housing Authority — MA
26. Portsmouth Housing Authority — VA
27. Port Huron Housing Commission — MI
28. Preston Housing Authority — CT
29. Providence Housing Authority — RI
30. Quincy Housing Authority — IL
31. Renton Housing Authority — WA
32. Rochester Housing Authority — NY
33. Shrewsbury Housing Authority — MA
34. Suffolk Housing Authority — VA
35. Sumter Housing Authority — SC
36. Tampa Housing Authority — FL
37. Visions of Oconto County — WI
38. Washtenaw Affordable Housing Corporation — MI
39. Waukegan Housing Authority — IL
40. Winchester Housing Authority — CT
41. Youngstown Metropolitan Housing Authority — OH

Appendix D: Defense Communities Magazine, Article about Safe-T-element® on Military Installations

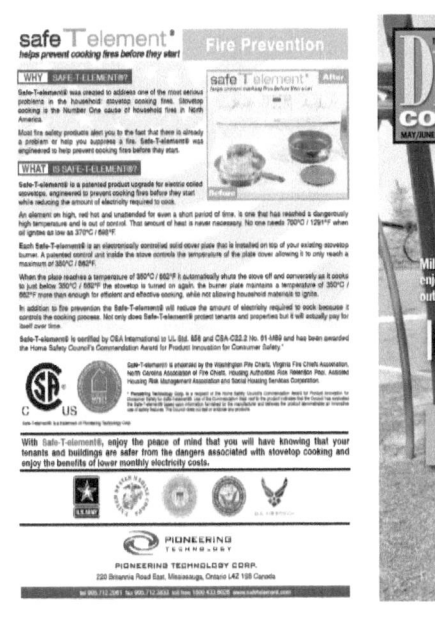

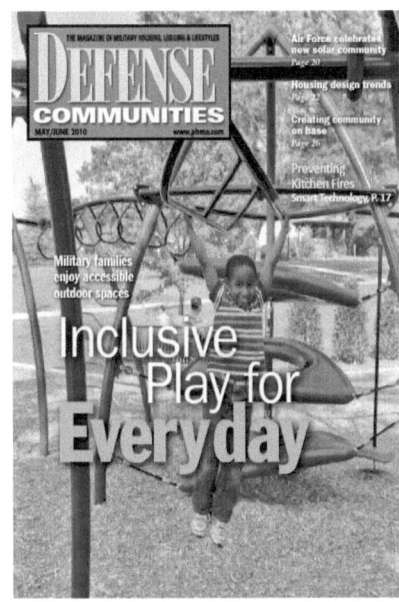

Appendix E: Pioneering Technology's Safe-T-element(R) installed in Washington State's King County Housing Authority (Press Release)

Pioneering Technology's Safe-T-element(R) to be installed in Washington State's King County Housing Authority thanks to $380,000 U.S. Department of Homeland Security Award

Safe-T-element identified as a leading solution to $billion stovetop kitchen fire problem at National Fire Prevention Strategy Meeting in Washington DC

MISSISSAUGA, ON, May 18 /CNW/ - Pioneering Technology Corp. of Mississauga, Ontario (TSX-V: PTE), ("Pioneering") announces today that it has been advised by the King County Housing Authority (KCHA) of Tukwila, Washington that they will be purchasing and installing the Safe-T-element cooking system in 2,000 of the KCHA's affordable housing units with a $381,300 grant from the Department of Homeland Security.

David Daniels, President of the King County Fire Chief's Association said in support of the KCHA's submission, "Since many of the KCHA's residential units do not have sprinkler systems, these fires can cause disastrous consequences resulting in the injury or death of tenants, staff and firefighters, as well as significant property damage. Elderly residents experiencing cognitive difficulties and those who lack experience with basic cooking safety precautions are compelling examples of KCHA residents who would benefit from this grant. I applaud King County Housing Authority for their efforts to ensure the safety of their residents by applying for this grant."

Pioneering CEO Kevin Callahan said of the announcement, "Homeland Security's ongoing commitment to this program is tremendous. This Washington State grant is a tribute to the KCHA and their efforts towards delivering a higher level of safety and energy efficiency to the people and the community they serve."

Other Homeland Security Safe-T-element award recipients announced so far this year include: the University of Miami; the Bellevue Washington Fire Department; Sandy Springs GA Fire Department; and the Norfolk Virginia Redevelopment and Housing Authority. Grants were awarded through the U.S. Department of

Homeland Security's Federal Emergency Management Agency's (FEMA) Fire Prevention and Safety grant program. Visit http://firegrantsupport.com for more information.

Pioneering due to its growing success as a solution provider of cooking related fire prevention technologies was recently invited to participate at the Vision 20/20 Strategy 4 Kitchen Fire Prevention Technologies Workshop inWashington DC. The Vision 20/20 National Forum was created to bring together some of the brightest minds in fire safety to develop a comprehensive national strategy for fire prevention in the United States. The goal of Vision 20/20 is to marshal forces for the development and support of a national strategic agenda for fire loss prevention. The workshop, by invitation only, was funded by the Department of Homeland Security, State Farm Insurance, and the Institute of Fire Engineers US Branch and included federal level government agencies, non-profit organizations, trade associations and stove manufacturers.

"We are very proud that our Safe-T-element technology was recently heralded as a leading technology that helps to prevent stovetop cooking fires at this national Fire Prevention Workshop in Washington, DC," said Callahan.

According to the National Fire Protection Association, stove top cooking fires are the number one cause of residential fires in North America and account for a disproportionate number of fires in apartment and affordable housing units. These fires caused an annual average 500 civilian deaths, 4,660 civilian injuries, and over a billion dollars in direct property damage. Pioneering's Safe-T-element is the only technology of its kind that helps prevent stovetop cooking fires from starting in the first place and has a proven track record in public, university, seniors and military housing facilities throughout North America.

For further information: regarding Pioneering Technology Corp. or the Safe-T-element cooking system contact: Kevin R. Callahan, President and CEO of Pioneering, at (905) 712-2061 ext. 222, or visit: www.pioneeringtech.com

Appendix F: Wilson, NC Ordinance Mandating Installation of HEHLT in all Tax-Supported Housing within City

O- 038-11

AN ORDINANCE TO THE CITY COUNCIL OF WILSON TO AMEND ARTICLE II, CHAPTER 14 (FIRE PREVENTION AND PROTECTION) OF THE CITY CODE TO MANDATE THE INSTALLATION OF LISTED AND APPROVED HIGH END HEAT LIMITING TECHNOLOGY ON ALL ELECTRIC COIL COOKING DEVICES LOCATED IN ALL TAX-SUPPORTED HOUSING WITHIN THE CITY OF WILSON'S JURISDICTION

BE IT ORDAINED by the City Council of the City of Wilson:

SECTION 1. That in Chapter 14 of the City Code, entitled "Fire Prevention and Protection", Article II, entitled "Fire Prevention Code" that a new subsection 14-47, entitled "Electric Cooking Devices in Tax-Supported Housing" be incorporated as follows:

All electric coil cooking devices in said housing shall be equipped with listed and approved high end heat limiting technology as recommended by the Fire Chief, or Authority Having Jurisdiction. Initial requirement will be for this technology on all new coil type electric ranges purchased for the purpose of replacement in existing housing, or as standard equipment for all new tax supported housing being built. All electric coil type ranges in all existing tax supported housing must comply with this requirement by the end of 2016.

Definitions:

1. Electric Coil Cooking Devices: All cooking devices that utilize a coil for the cooking heat source. This includes free standing and built in electric ranges, "drop in" type counter-top cook tops and hot plates.
2. High End Heat Limiting Technology: A device that is hard wired into the electric coil range (tamper proof) that limits the high end cooking temperature to a safe level that prevents auto-ignition of common cooking and household materials.
3. Tax Supported Housing: Any housing that is initially constructed by, and/or rent subsidized by the taxpayers for the purpose of providing affordable housing for the at-need citizens within the City of Wilson's jurisdiction. Also included are privately owned properties for the purpose of rental, in which the rent is subsidized by the taxpayers.

SECTION 2. That this ordinance may be enforced by any one, all, or a combination of the remedies authorized.

Appendix G: Sandy Springs, GA, Press Release Regarding HEHLT Technology

'Tis the Season: One department's quest to reduce cooking fires

By David L. Adams, R.A. CFO, CBO

If your department is like most, you respond to a lot of cooking fires, and the number of calls for them goes way up during the holidays. According to the NFPA, firefighters encounter three times as many cooking fires on Thanksgiving than on an average day—and cooking equipment fires are the leading cause of U.S. home fires and fire injuries, and the third leading cause of fire deaths.

Although we must be prepared to respond to the higher call volume for these incidents during the holidays, we also need to ask ourselves, what preventive measures can we take to reduce the number of cooking fires throughout the year? With the help of a grant and some new technology, my department is hoping to do just that.

On Oct. 31, 2007, this fire broke out on Winding River Road in Sandy Springs, caused by unattended cooking. The top floor and contents were nearly totaled (four apartments), and the lower floor and contents received tremendous water damage.

On May 18, 2009, at 7600 Roswell Road, fire destroyed eight apartments and caused extensive water damage to an additional four apartments. Although the cause was officially undetermined, unattended cooking was a likely cause.

Quick Facts: Sandy Springs (Ga.) Fire Department

The Sandy Springs Fire Department's service area includes a residential population of approximately 98,000 and a daytime population
that has been estimated to swell to 125,000. The department has 91 full-time firefighters to respond to an average annual call volume of 7,000.

Compounding matters, the department has 43,000 housing units (92% are occupied and 59% are multi-family dwellings) with a median value of $316,000 within its densely populated boundary. The service area also includes some of the most desirable commercial corporate high-rise buildings (e.g., UPS Corporate, Newell Rubbermaid, Cox Enterprises) in the nation.

Project STOP

The Sandy Springs (Ga.) Fire Department response area includes 73 apartment complexes and a total of 43,000 housing units (92% are occupied and 59% are multi-family dwellings). An informal assessment using data from fire incident reports, along with the observations of fire service personnel, revealed that cooking fires are a large problem within the community (see sidebar photos for some specific incidents).

Ordinary elements (Before) and the Safe-T-Element® (After)

Our assessment also indicated that a large percentage of these fires occur in apartment buildings and among vulnerable populations (defined as seniors above the age of 65 and "latchkey" children who range from ages 12 to 16 and are likely to cook alone while their parents or primary care person are working). Accordingly, our department has implemented a strategy of education and technology that is focused on one of our greatest target hazards: rental apartments.

On Aug. 7, 2009, our city received a $38,000 federal grant to launch a program to address this issue specifically and fire safety more broadly. The grant help started Project STOP, which educates at-risk seniors and young children on reducing the occurrence of cooking fires and the necessary action steps to take during a fire. The course was developed from a teaching outline developed by FEMA and NFPA.

Project STOP includes two main elements:

1. Promote fire prevention and safety through targeted education presentations for seniors and children, given that they reside in apartment complexes prone to cooking fires.

2. Install safety equipment during the site visits. Combined, these two strategies will go a long way in protecting the community against potential deaths, injuries and property damage, not to mention mitigating the risks faced by seniors and "latchkey" children.

Prevention through Technology

The safety equipment installed as part of Project STOP includes new technology developed to address unattended cooking fires (NFPA estimates 90% of cooking fires result from food left unattended): Safe-T-Element is a technology that prevents common combustibles from igniting and burning on the stovetop. An electric element on a typical electric range will heat to about 1,300–1,600 degrees F; common combustibles generally ignite and burn at about 700 degrees F.

A temperature-control device that prevents the element from reaching these temperatures eliminates all stovetop fires, including cooking oil fires.

Recent multiple-loss tragedies due to unattended cooking in Charlotte and Atlanta remind us that stovetop cooking fires represent the largest cause of home fires. NFIRS data states that cooking fires were responsible for about 80 deaths, 3,875 injuries and $481 million in property loss in the United States in 2002. Project STOP will provide high-risk target groups with proven and effective prevention messages and safety equipment to mitigate the risk and occurrence of cooking fires.

The holidays provide an opportunity to educate the public about the dangers associated with cooking fires. But programs like Project STOP ensure that the education continues year-round, and the latest technology is deployed to further protect those most at-risk.

David L. Adams, RA, CBO, CFO, is the fire protection engineer with the Sandy Springs Fire Department. Feel free to contact David at 770/206-2083 or david.adams@sandyspringsga.org.

Appendix H: NFPA, Fire Analysis and Research, U.S. Home Structure Fires Fact Sheet

Fire Analysis and Research

U.S. Home Structure Fires Fact Sheet

U.S. fire departments responded to an estimated average of 366,600 home structure[1] fires per year during 2007-2011. These fires caused an annual average of

> 2,570 civilian fire deaths,
> 13,210 civilian fire injuries, and
> $7.2 billion in direct damage.

- 92% of all structure fire deaths resulted from home fires.

- On average, seven people died in U.S. home fires per day.

Causes and Circumstances of Home Fires

Cooking equipment was the leading cause of home structure fires and home fire injuries.

Smoking was the leading cause of civilian home fire deaths. Heating equipment was the second most common cause of home fire fatalities.

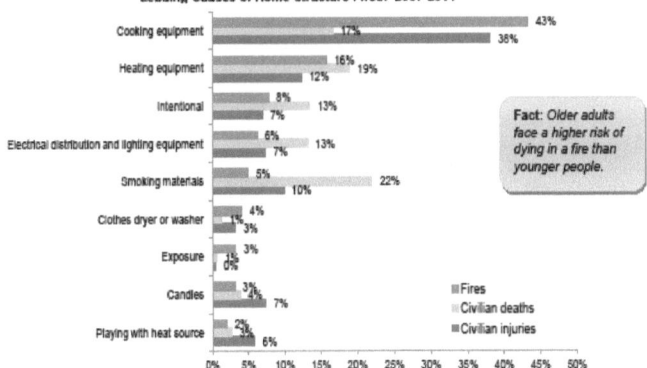

Leading Causes of Home Structure Fires: 2007-2011

Fact: Older adults face a higher risk of dying in a fire than younger people.

Almost all homes have at least one smoke alarm, but three out of five home fire deaths in 2007-2011 resulted from fires in homes in which no smoke alarm was present (37%) or at least one was present but none operated (23%).

[1]Homes include one- or two-family homes, manufactured homes, as well as apartments or other multi-family housing. In general, any fire that occurs in or in a structure is considered a structure fire, even if the fire was limited to contents and the building itself was not damaged. Estimates were derived from USFA's National Fire Incident Reporting System and NFPA's annual fire department experience survey.

Appendix I: But Wait, There's More! (Technology for the Microwave Oven)

Pioneering Technology, makers of the safe-T-element™, has also created a technology solution for fires that originate in microwave ovens. The safe-T-sensor™, is a patent pending technology designed to detect burning conditions within the microwave and to shut the microwave off before it causes a fire or triggers the fire alarm.

safe T sensor™   **HELPS PREVENT MICROWAVE FIRES & FALSE ALARMS**

WHY SAFE-T-SENSOR™ ?

Safe-T-sensor™ will help prevent most fires, fire alarm activations and the related fire department responses for problems caused by microwave ovens.

FACT:
● Microwave ovens are involved in an estimated 6600 home fires each year resulting in 3 deaths, 110 injuries and $22 million in direct property damage. *Source: NFPA*
● Microwaves used improperly and left unattended result in tens of thousands of false alarms, building evacuations, fire department responses and tenant apathy.

SOLUTION: The Safe-T-sensor™ was created to substantially reduce fire alarm activations caused by microwave ovens by interrupting power to the microwave at the first sign of smoke.

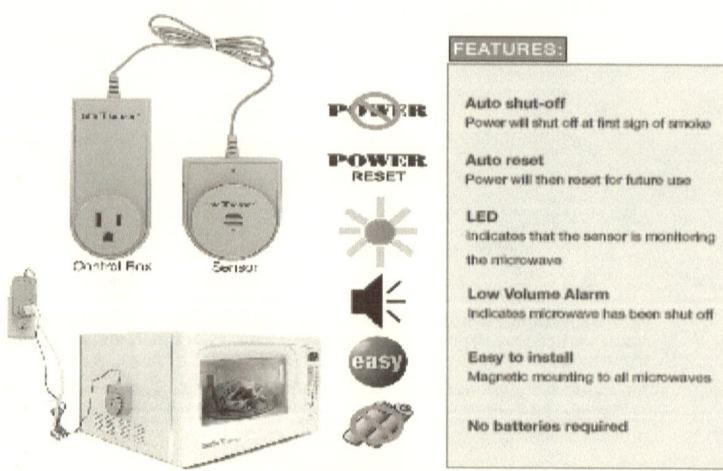

FEATURES:

Auto shut-off
Power will shut off at first sign of smoke

Auto reset
Power will then reset for future use

LED
Indicates that the sensor is monitoring the microwave

Low Volume Alarm
Indicates microwave has been shut off

Easy to install
Magnetic mounting to all microwaves

No batteries required

PIONEERING TECHNOLOGY

PIONEERING TECHNOLOGY CORP.
220 Britannia Road East, Mississauga, Ontario, L4Z 1S6 Canada
tel 905.712.2061 fax 905.712.3635 toll free 1.800.433.6026 www.pioneeringtech.com

A study completed by Ohio University's Environmental Health and Safety (EHS) and the Athens Ohio Fire Department (AFD) found that the majority of the fire department's nuisance alarms on campus were caused by burnt food in microwave ovens.

It was estimated that there was a direct cost of more than $2,000 for each run AFD made to campus. The campus experiences well over 100 AFD nuisance runs per year. Since the summer of 2009 the EHS department at Ohio University has been keeping statistical records of all fire runs to campus by the AFD.

PIONEERING
TECHNOLOGY

The Problem:

Microwave oven related cooking fires and false alarms are one of the most persistent and significant fire related problems in University campus residence halls and or dorm rooms across the country.

According to the National Fire Protection Association (NFPA), microwave ovens are involved in 2,100 home structure fires per year and are responsible for more emergency room injury visits than any other cooking device.

And while microwave oven fires are of great concern the numbers are relatively low as compared to the number of false alarms/nuisance calls created by the accidental misuse of this appliance in college dorms. For example, a student puts a package of popcorn in the microwave oven and then accidentally hits 20 minutes instead of 2 minutes and then leaves the dorm room. The result is a very smoky situation that results in a fire alarm. The fire alarm then results in the evacuation of the building and a fire department response and this is where the real danger exists. Specifically:

> ➤ Evacuations related to alarms create dangerous situations;
> ➤ Fire trucks driving through university campuses create dangerous situations for students and firefighters;
> ➤ Fire related nuisance responses cost the university and the city a great deal of money per response;
> ➤ After the 2nd or 3rd time an alarm goes off in the middle of the night students stop getting out of bed...
> ➤ ... And this is when things get really dangerous.

"When I hear the alarm go off, I tend to shrug it off or sigh because it's almost never real,"
- Ohio University sophomore student

---

safe T sensor™   Case Study – University Housing

"Microwave cooking related fire runs/nuisance calls reduced by 92%"

OHIO
UNIVERSITY

Ohio University, established in 1804, is one of the oldest and most respected public educational institutions in the United States. Ohio University has an enrollment of over 32,000 students on all campuses. The main campus in Athens has 17,245 undergraduate students and 3,595 graduate students. Residential Housing consists of a housing system of 42 residence halls across three residential greens that house nearly 8,000 students.

45

The Solution:

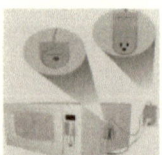

The Safe-T-sensor, developed by Pioneering is the only technology of its kind that helps mitigate the many fires and false alarms attributed to the use of microwave ovens. The Safe-T-sensor is a patent pending technology designed to detect burning conditions within the microwave and to shut the microwave off before it causes a fire or triggers the fire alarm.

- The smoke "sensor" is attached magnetically to the microwave.
- The microwave plugs into the "control box" which is plugged into the outlet.
- The solution is simple, seamless and requires no change to cooking behavior.

It was determined by Ohio University that if the Safe-T-sensors could eliminate about 100 runs over a three-year period, the resulting savings in time and money would be significant for everyone involved.

In August 2010, Ohio University purchased 4,630 Safe-T-sensors to be installed in residence halls to help reduce the occurrence of nuisance fire alarms and the associated runs by AFD to university housing facilities. The University hoped that the Safe-T-sensors would reduce AFD's nuisance runs to residence halls by 75 percent. Ohio installed the first 3,593 sensors in December during the schools winter break. Classes resumed January 3, 2011. Educational presentations were given to residential staff and materials were presented to all students receiving the sensors.

The Results:

In the first 14 weeks of 2010 the AFD responded to the University 38 times. Of those 38 runs 10 were burnt food in microwave ovens that activated the buildings fire system resulting in an evacuation. During the same 14 weeks of 2011, in the same residential halls with Safe-T-sensors installed, the AFD responded to campus 28 times with 1 being related to burnt food in a microwave oven. **The result of the Safe-T-sensor installations and the corresponding cooking fire safety education was a 92% reduction in same type runs to campus compared to 2010.**

Ohio University believes that the education provided at the time of installation not only helped reduce the number of burnt microwave food alarms but resulted in a greater awareness of fire safety as reflected by the reduction of total runs for the first quarter of 2011. The University has now installed 4,479 sensors and the University expects this trend to continue.

The Ohio University staff of Environmental Health and Safety plans to continue its efforts and ongoing education to new students each year to stress the importance of these devices and of the awareness of fire safety.

"The investment in these sensors has reduced fire runs, response hazards, late night residence evacuations, interruption in study time and the cost of fire equipment operation, campus police and personnel required to investigate"
- Brent Auker – Fire Protection Engineer, Ohio University

Pioneering Technology that Protects Properties, Reduces Energy and Saves Lives.

Pioneering Technology Corp. (TSX-V:PTE)	
220 Britannia Road East	Phone: 905.712.2061 x230
Mississauga, Ontario, Canada L4Z 1S6	Toll-Free: 800.433.7026 x230
info@pioneeringtech.com	Fax: 905.712.3833
www.pioneeringtech.com	www.safetsensor.com

PIONEERING
TECHNOLOGY

Pioneering Technology Corp.
220 Britannia Road East
Mississauga, Ontario,
Canada L4Z IS6

April 21, 2011.

Kevin Callahan:

Ohio University purchased 4,630 Safe-T-Sensors in 2010 from University Electronics to install in the residential halls on campus. During winter break 3,593 sensors were installed. Classes resumed January 3, 2011. Educational presentations were given to residential staff and materials presented to all students receiving the sensors.

Since summer of 2009 Environmental Health and Safety began keeping statistical records of all fire runs to campus by Athens Fire Department. Using these statistics provided good information to validate fire safety improvements. These statistics were used to compare the first 14 weeks of 2011 against the same time in 2010. These records only reflect the residential halls that have had sensors installed. In 2010 The Athens Fire Department responded to the university 38 times in the first 14 weeks. Of those 38 runs 10 were burnt food in microwave ovens that set off a smoke detector and activated the buildings fire system. During the same 14 weeks of 2011 in the same residential halls with Safe-T-sensors; the Athens Fire Department responded to campus for 28 runs with 2 being burnt food in microwave ovens. Of these 2 incidents one sensor was found to have been moved and the second was replaced because it was uncertain of why it failed. This was a 92% reduction in same type runs to campus compared to 2010.

We also feel that the education we have provided to everyone involved contributed to better awareness of fire safety .It appears to reflect this by reduction of total runs for first quarter of 2011. Installation of all 4,479 sensors has been completed as of April 2011. By the end of this school year the numbers should still reflect a 90% decrease in burnt food related fire runs. The investment in the purchase of the sensors through a federal grant along with time for EHS staff to install these units has paid off in various ways. It has reduced fire runs, hazards associated with response, evacuation of resident halls at all hours, interruption of study time, total cost for fire equipment operation and campus police and personnel needed to investigate the cause of the alarms.

The staff of Environmental Health and Safety will continue its efforts in ongoing education to new students each year to stress the importance of these devices and of the awareness of fire safety. We would like to thank the all those involved in helping us achieve these goals.

Brent Auker
Fire Protection Engineer
Ohio University
Athens, Ohio 45701